Tantric Sex: The Truth About Tantric Sex

The Ultimate Beginner's Guide to Sacred Sexuality Through Neotantra

Table Of Contents

Introduction

In this short and concise book, you will learn what tantric sex is all about. We will go into its origin, the Tantra lifestyle, and how you can use helpful techniques to improve your sexual relations with your partner.

This book aims to let you experience the most satisfying, magical, and sacred form of the sexual act. It brings to light the things you need to know and practice in order to achieve the ultimate sexual experience.

We are not advocating the practice of tantric sex, per se, but we want to make sure that if someone is interested in this controversial topic, he or she can reach more informed conclusions.

We hope that you are able to learn a thing or two from reading this!

Chapter 1:

What Is Tantric Sex?

Human sex has been in existence for as long as humans have inhabited the earth. However, many people are too embarrassed to even talk about it, even with their partners.

Practically every adult knows what sex means. However, some find it taboo. There seems to be an unwritten rule that says you cannot talk about sex in public and, for some people, even in private.

Sex is supposed to be sacred, because it is a union between two people who love each other and who want to become and live as one. It is the ultimate expression of one's love and passion for another.

This book is about a sacred form of sexuality – tantric sex. It is one of the oldest philosophies of spiritual sexuality, but it is still being practiced to this very day.

Sexuality is more than just pro-creation — and tantric sex will help you understand that. As you continue to improve at it, you may even find yourself becoming more imaginative, playful, and creative as a person.

What is Tantra?

Before discussing tantric sex, there are several terms that need to be learned before we can understand what this kind of sexual experience is all about.

Tantra is a Sanskrit word. The prefix *tan* means "to expand, weave, or join," while the suffix *tra* means "tool." The definition of the word *tantra* is "a tool to liberate, to bring together, and to expand." Tantra is more than 1,500 years old and originated in India, just like yoga. Its teachings are designed to help people feel more and to increase awareness of one's own energy and the energy around them. The path to be used is the exploration of the sexual energy.

Tantric sex's role, therefore, is to allow you to experience the full depth that your sexuality has to offer, because sex is more than just physical pleasure and satisfaction. In "traditional sex," the goal is to achieve ultimate satisfaction and ecstasy, referred to as an orgasm, but in tantric sex, the end goal is enriching one's entire sexual experience with his/her partner.

Tantra is not a religion, nor is it affiliated with any religious groups or beliefs. Even if its traditional teachings are based on the precepts of "universal energy" and "higher power," it is not confined to just one set of rules, religious teachings, or beliefs. If you are considering the concept that sacred sexual expression will bring you closer to a "higher power," then practicing the tantra is a powerful option.

Tantra can also help you establish a deeper sexual connection with your partner. It's beauty is that it offers a lot of wonderful things, without having to follow a specific set of rules and/or beliefs.

Is Tantric Sex for Everyone?

Most of the teachings in tantra are all about expressing your desires and experiencing enhanced sexual energy. There is no mention of improving your sex life or enhancing your sexual libido, similar to the typical western approaches to sex. Tantra teachings are not focused on the physical aspects of how your body looks, how you wear your hair, what car you drive, or where you live. Tantric sex is open to anyone and everyone interested in exploring a different path to achieve sexual fulfillment.

Tantric sex is not limited by gender, age, or sexual orientation, because it is for everyone who wants to further improve their sex life and, at the same time, get in touch with their souls and the souls of their partners.

The Chakras

Part of the teachings of tantra is recognizing the different energy systems that are within the human body – within you. One of the most commonly known energy systems are the chakras, wherein energy is centered in the body, between the pelvis and the top of the head. With this system of thought, the concept is that the smooth energy flow in your body can get stuck somewhere in the system due to blockages or depletion.

Practicing tantric sex will help in the continuous flow of energy.It helps facilitate the normal and smooth flow of energy.

The Sacral Chakra

It is said that the Sacral Chakra, also known as the Sexual Chakra, has a lot to do with opening a person to tantric sex. This is because the Sacral Chakra is home to sexual and creative energies that help improve your relationships with other people and your ability to nurture life. Your Sacral Chakra is able to tap into the following:

Your conscious sexuality

The Yin-Yang Balance of Your Sacred
Masculine/Feminine Dance

Your sexuality and who you really are during the
most intimate moments

Basically, this chakra distributes sexual energy to your entire body as needed. It also has a lot to do with issues of power in the outside world. When you are in tune with your sexuality and your intimacy as a whole, you become more confident in yourself. This way, your dreams and desires will also be manifested easier — without having a hard time pressing those issues. That said, here's what you need to know about the Sacral Chakra:

It is found just below the navel, around 5 centimeters below it, and just near the pubis as well.

It is represented by the color Orange. Recently, the color Indigo has also been associated with it and has been deemed to represent unlimited manifestation.

Its main affirmations include: *I deserve, I feel, I want.*

Its functions include: sexuality, pleasure, procreation, emotions, and creativity, waking up the subconscious, relationships, self-gratification, imagination, movement, and sensations.

In Sanskrit, it is called *Svadhistana,* which literally means "One's own abode" or "sweetness."

In the Endocrine System, it is located near the gonads and ovaries.

As for physical organs, it provides amazing benefits for the kidneys, reproductive system, bladder, and circulatory organs.

As for body parts, it provides great benefits for the hips, lower back, genitals, large intestine, urinary tract, prostate, and lower digestive organs.

Sacral Chakra can also improve one's tastebuds.

It can also be tapped into by gemstones, such as Orange Calcite, Carnelian, Red Tiger's Eye, and Sunstone.

Tantric Sex

The stereotypical western world's concept of sex is like telling a story with a clear beginning (which is sexual excitement), then the middle (the penetration), and the ultimate end (which is reaching orgasm). For a lot of people, they believe that this is the pattern that everyone should follow. If the "procedure" is not followed, something might be wrong, or the sexual act could be wrong. For most couples, sexual intercourse without penetration is not real sex - it is simply foreplay.

With tantric sex, the end goal is not orgasm, as the main focus is letting you feel the experience of being intimate with someone. Tantric sex has no beginning, no middle, and no end. The exercises used to practice the tantra include slowing things down, diverting your focus from the external body, and paying attention to what goes on in your soul.

Tantric sex is not all about achieving orgasm, because its main goal is to increase awareness of yourself. You don't need to feel pressured to do it the "right" way or to be self-conscious, regarding whichever positions you and your partner adopt. Nevertheless, don't assume that you cannot reach orgasm when you practice tantric sex. In fact, you can even achieve multiple and longer orgasms!

Chapter 2:

History of Tantric Sex

Since the beginning, humankind has struggled with defining the concept of sexuality and intimacy. However, there are sciences and forms of art that are aimed at honoring the sacredness of sex and sexuality.

Look at it this way: the universe and its origins are rooted in the fusion, or becoming as one, of the creative energies in both human and cosmic forms. All of the sacred thought systems have different concepts of the female and male creative energies. Furthermore, it cannot be denied that every major philosophy and religion attempts to shed some light on the nature of human sexual energy. They often involve looking to find the answers in order to better understand and explore the deeper concepts of sacred sex and the "marriage" of sexuality and spirituality.

The practice of tantric sex dates back to the ancient culture of the *Lemurians*. There is no written proof of their sexual practices, as everything they did, their methods, and other ownerships were only transferred through their descendants from generation to generation. It is believed that the early inhabitants of Hawaii are the only known descendants of the *Lemurians*.

Nonetheless, our ancestors have been said to have used spirituality, aromatherapy, vibrational healing, and creativity. Everybody lived as one with the body and soul, and they honored the feminine and creative aspects of human life. The *Lemurians* were also said to be the first people to practice the healing art, *Reiki*, which is still being practiced today. The preserved arts of sacred sexuality are believed to be in the form of the Taoist Art of Sexology and the Tantra.

Whatever the name given to the sacred art of sexuality, the concepts will always remain the same - it is rooted in the belief that the sacred art of sexuality is practiced with the main purpose of transforming humankind's mundane feelings, thoughts, and energy to a spiritualized, higher, personal experience of oneness, and union with everything in existence.

The Tantra

As mentioned earlier, Tantra is the oldest sacred art
of sexuality known to humankind, and it is still being
practiced to this day. The origins of the Tantra are not
clear, though. There are different versions, including
one that says Tantra is a disciplined system from
Hinduism. Other historians say Tantra came from the
Buddhist monks. Still, others insist that Tantra was
developed from the communities in the East Indian
villages.

There are other so-called experts who believe yoga
and Tantra are one and the same. However, the main
purpose of yoga is to cultivate self-awareness and
higher consciousness, while the Tantra is all about
weaving together and liberation of the body.
Considering the fact that most of the physically
challenging positions of tantric sex are known to be

yoga postures, these experts concluded that even if Tantra is not yoga, it is patterned after yoga.

What the modern world knows about Tantra is that its most common form is preserved in some popular ancient writings, like *Kama Sutra* (assumed to have been written around the time of Christ) and the *Ananga Ranga* (a collection of erotic writings, first published in 1100 A.D.).

A noble man is attributed to have authored the *Kama Sutra*. He saw life as comprising of the *dharma*, or spiritual substance, the *artha*, or financial substance, and *Kama*, or sensual substance.

Kama is known as the "enjoyment of appropriate objects through the five senses, being assisted by the mind and the soul." Tantra may appear to be the art of sexual pleasuring and *Kama Sutra* is a collection of sexual positions. The main purpose of *Kama* is to cultivate love and develop worship and veneration for the body of one's partner.

When you look at the Tantric experience, it is easy to assume you will be experiencing "great sexual intercourse." However, if it is seen and experienced beyond the physical aspect (clairvoyantly), then it is actually an astonishing dance and display of color and energy, nothing close to experiencing an epic display of fireworks.

Opening the Sacral Chakra

In order to get yourself ready for tantric sex, you should first learn to open the Sacral Chakra. You can do this by following the guidelines below:

Spend time near open waters and under the moonlight. This will help you feel and appreciate healthy flowing mechanisms in your own body.

Try to surround yourself with beauty. For example: flowers, color, art, and music — or just about anything that makes you feel happy and makes you appreciate your role in this world even further.

Try to use perfumes with sandalwood, musk, or ylang-ylang. These open the Sacral Chakra more than any other scents.

You can also repeat the following affirmations to yourself:

I am giving myself permission to enjoy my sexuality.

I know that pleasure is an important, sacred part of my life.

Being able to enjoy sex and sensuality brings me joy and nourishes my spirit.

I am allowing my emotions to fill me in a good way.

My life is pleasurable and graceful.

The tantric sexual experience is divided into the following three stages:

Physical

The main focus is on the physical pleasure you are experiencing in that particular moment. Listed below are some of the ways that can help you experience physical tantric sex:

Stop talking.

Just allow yourselves to get lost in the moment. Intimacy is not just about the dirty talk; sometimes, it is also about the silence — how you'd allow yourselves to just focus on the moment and not think or talk about anything for a couple of minutes (preferably even longer over time).

Try to slow it down.

Undress each other. Focus on each part of the body, instead of going rough right away. In order to enjoy the beauty of intimacy, you have to learn every single part of your partner's body. You have to enjoy the beauty of undressing each other and the joy you get from foreplay. Take your time — there is nothing wrong with that.

Enjoy sex without orgasms.

Sometimes, you only get intimate, because you're looking forward to the orgasm(s). However, there are also times when you should learn to enjoy foreplay alone and understand that even without orgasms, sex can still be an incredibly beautiful experience for you and your partner.

Breathe life into it.

This means that you also have to focus on the way you and your partner breathe. It can be sexy to just hear the sound of your partner's breaths; you now breathe the same air, and you help each other get lost in the moment. Improving this has the potential to make sex purely magical.

Emotional

Emotional tantric sex typically refers to deeply invoking amorous thoughts and "worshiping" each other's divinity. This means you have to create an emotional connection in bed. Here's how you can work on this:

Try to say what you want to happen.

No, you don't have to do this while you're already in bed and on the way to making love, but you can talk about it while having dinner and the like. Sometimes, it's important to tell your partner what you want to happen — for example, those sexual fantasies that you've always had — so that he/she can also think of ways to make the fantasy happen. Make sure it is a two-way street: learn how to give in to your partner's needs as well.

Recognize your emotional experiences with your partner.

Remember how you feel when you realize just how much you love your partner. Try to tap into the deepest parts of your heart and see how you really feel about this person. Intimacy isn't just about what you get to share physically, but how you know each other by heart.

Remember that neither of you are perfect.

Sometimes, you expect so much from your partner that you forget to realize he/she is only able to fulfill your desires if you are communicating properly. Make your expectations realistic, and do not wish for something that you know you cannot give. Always work to improve the communication skills and the dynamic that the two of you have.

Look each other in the eyes.

In order to be aware of a strong emotional connection, it is important to learn how to look into each other's eyes during sex. By getting better at this, you'll notice just how differently you and your partner feel, as compared to just practicing "normal" or rough sex.

Try to assess how you feel about your partner in a sexual context.

Are you excited to be intimate with your partner? What do you want to do with him/her, and how do you think intimacy would improve your relationship in the long run?

Spiritual

Spiritual tantric sex typically means feeling each other as one, connected to the "Supreme Being" or "God." And finally, you have the spiritual component, which a lot of people consider to be one of the most important parts of tantric sex. You can make it work this way:

Remember that sex isn't just a union of bodies; it is a union of two people.

In short, you both really have to be into the act for tantric sex to be practiced and achieved. The powerful, ecstatic feelings that one can feel in the prime of a tantric sexual experience do not come from "forcing" the act or consciously trying to manipulate the other person. It must be allowed through the combination of two people, trusting and being in touch with each other (no pun intended).

Move beyond self-absorption and narcissism.

Always treat your partner fairly. Sexual spirituality begins when you both achieve a kind of maturity that does not rely on narcissism or in making each other feel less than what you're supposed to feel. As a couple, you have a life that is shared by the two of you—and it's important to recognize this is the top priority, even in times of sexual intercourse.

Step outside reality.

You don't have to think of every single problem you
have while in bed with your partner. You just have to
think of the moment. Focus on leaving your problems
outside of the sexual experience. In essence, tantric
sex can be a type of meditational session if done
correctly.

Sex can be virtuous without being prudish.

Sex can be clean, without one of you feeling like a prude. This happens when you both agree on what you want to happen — and how you want it to happen.

Tantric sex is also a form of prayer.

Why? Because it invokes the deepest parts of your soul and helps you to be in tune with another person. When you pray, it's not just about wishing for what's good for you; it's also about caring for others, and that's how sex should be as well.

Aside from mystical and cosmic experiences, most Tantric masters also look for deeper and more personal experiences with other people and the world in which they live. They believe that if there is deep interconnection, then the formerly perceived space between two people will be replaced with the light of the Supreme Being. They believe this spiritual presence activates the etheric energy between two people, thus "weaving them together" so they can become one.

They believe Tantra is actually a divine path that has to be practiced with the utmost divinity and sacredness. Tantra is supposed to be practiced as if one were engaging in a spiritual "ritual", and like most spiritual worship, it is inevitable to honor and acknowledge the Supreme Being. However, in this ideology, when you are practicing tantric sex, the deity is actually embodied in your partner instead of a vague image.

Tantra is never an abstract form of any saintly or holy practice, but it is actually a practical practice in which the experience with the Supreme Being is being sent to the deepest realms of your senses. This doesn't mean, though, that you cannot practice all the other forms of worship or spirituality. The challenge of Tantra to all lovers is to feel, see, and hear the presence of the Supreme Being when they are being joined together as one during Tantric lovemaking.

Two Paths of Training

There are two paths in the practice of the Tantra: *vama-marga*, or the left-hand path, and *dakshina-marga*, or the right-hand path.

Vama-Marga

Vama-marga is more about practicing Tantra by way of performing actual sexual intercourse, complete with penetration and an orgasmic experience. The left-hand path practices the maithuna ritual, *"The Five Makaras."*

In the evening, a number of practitioners will participate in performing and receiving five symbols of pleasure:

Madya: Wine

Matsya: Fish

Mamsa: Meat

Mudra: Parched Grain

Maithuna: Sacred Sex

This means you have to make use of tantric sex positions in order to understand what tantric sex can really do, and how it can make the two of you feel. It also means you have to follow simple guidelines before and while having sex. These include:

You should come together and decide what you want to happen and when you want it to take place. For a while, you can gaze into each other's eyes while sitting together in silence. Breathe in and breathe out in synchrony.

Now, speak to each other and talk about how you're going to get through this. Decide whether or not this will be orgasmic.

Get into it. Eventually, you will be able to develop your own pace and style, and your energies as partners will begin to work in harmony. For example, instead of thrusting, you can start rocking. Or, maybe you could use your hands and fingers to play with each others' bodies. You can also think of a "speed limit" or just how long you'll have sex — this is a good way of creating friction, making the act intense, and making sure that you both make the most of it.

Let the genital sensations flow through your body. Let yourself get lost in them.

Make way for stillness. It's like deciding to stay the course and hold each other when one of you feels lost or when the moment becomes too overwhelming.

Use full deep breaths. Research has shown that deep breathing makes way for better arousal. Why? Well, because laborious breathing always feels real. By doing so, you both know that you're into what you're doing, and of course, that can help both of you feel fantastic.

Try running cycles of erotic changes. This means you can be creative and adventurous with what you are doing in bed. You can be creative by imagining the feeling of your juices coming together, and this could help magnify your communion as a couple.

Last, remember that sex should equate to making love. As a couple, sex should bring you closer together. It shouldn't just feel like a job. It should be like a communion of souls, something fragile, yet beautiful, at the same time.

Dakshima-Marga

On the other hand, *Dakshina-marga* practices the symbolic Tantra, wherein partners view their intercourse as telling a story. There are certain ways for Dakshima-Marga to be invoked, and it could be one or a few of the following:

There could be a guru-disciple relationship.

For example, one of you could introduce tantric sex to the other. Then, both of you would not be at a loss at the same time — otherwise, you may not be able to create a great sexual experience.

Try going to tantric classes.

By attending tantric classes, you'd be able to make use of empowerments given by tantric masters, which will help you learn how you can attain certain aspects of the mind and make sure the practices you'll make won't be dangerous for your health. This way, the experiences wouldn't be "half-assed" and would actually feel complete for both people.

Make use of Dharanis.

Dharanis work like Mantras, but are more specific. In some cases, they are not meant to be understood by others. They are mantras that you create and utter only for yourself, not because you're selfish, but because you want something to happen the way you want it to happen.

Repeat Mantras.

These are the simple ones that you could utter in your daily life or can write in journals or notepads. It's all about making sure you know what you want and how you want it to happen. By communicating what you want to your partner, he/she may start to crave giving you the fantasy that you want in his/her own mantra.

Try Pranayama (breath control), Yantra (mystical diagrams), and Trul Khor Yoga.

Pranayama

Pranayama is a form of a breath control exercise that you can use to invoke Dakshima-Marga. Here's a simple exercise that you can follow:

Use your thumb and index finger to pinch your eyebrows.

Massage your temples.

Pull your ears for at least 10-15 seconds. The reason for doing this is simple: Yogis believe that doing so is a sign that says, no other person will be able to "pull your ears" or bring you down!

Close your eyes then open them wide. Use your fingers to pull them wide and do so 10-15 times.

Massage your chin and cheeks by using your first, middle, and ring fingers.

Move your ears clockwise and counter-clockwise.

For around 8-10 repetitions, move your jaw throughout its full range of motion.

Take a few deep breaths and move your head up and down slowly in sync with your diaphragm.

For the aforementioned practices, make sure you follow these guidelines as well:

Make sure you do this while you are in a calm state.

There's no need to overdo it - 4-5 minutes is okay.

Try to prevent yourself from feeling self-conscious. Embrace the exercises without judging.

Use the power of imagination while thinking about how your body is moving.

Make these practices a part of your daily routine.

Yantras

Yantras are mystical diagrams that you can get from tantric masters or even certain websites that will help calm your mind a bit. The prime example is an adult coloring book (mandala).

It's important to make use of yantras, because they develop your expressions; they'll help you listen to your mind and soul even further, forcing you to keep your mind open, rather than focusing on the superficial in which we can get caught.

Trul Khol Yoga

Trul Khol Yoga is also known as "Sexual Yoga" —
which could, of course, open your mind to tantric
sex. Here are some exercises you can try:

Lingering Breath

1. Sit down on the floor in a cross-legged position.

2. Inhale slowly and exhale at the count of 5.

3. Inhale for another 5 counts and exhale the same way.

4. Continue for at least 3 sets.

Yogi Sit-Up

1. Sit with your knees together on the floor, and then bend your torso.

2. Now, lift your feet up until your shins are parallel to the floor and make sure your knees are still bent.

3. Raise up your palms and make sure they are level with your knees.

4. Count to five, exhale, and then lower your legs towards the floor.

5. Exhale and get back to the starting position.

The Frog

1. Place your elbows and forearms on the floor.

2. Start by walking with your hands on your knees, and then exhale slowly and press your hips back until you feel a stretch in your inner thighs.

3. Hold for around 5 seconds, release, and repeat.

The Triangle

1. Extend your arms to the sides and then bend your right leg.

2. Now, stand with your feet at least 3 feet apart with the toes on the right side at a 90-degree angle.

3. Look up to the ceiling and hold for around 5 breaths.

4. Stand and repeat the exercise on the opposite side of your body.

Bridge with Kegel

1. Lie with your knees bent on your back, and keep your heels and butt as close together as possible.

2. Place your arms on the floor with your palms facing down and with your fingertips pointing towards your heels.

3. Press your feet towards the floor and exhale before pushing your hips towards the ceiling.

4. Lower your hips to the floor and repeat for at least 2 more repetitions.

Past and Present

When you read some of the ancient Tantric writings, a woman's sexual experience and spiritual energy are referred to as the *Shakti*. In Hinduism, the goddess *Shakti* is a representation of the female principle of energy. While S*hakti* exists in both men and women, the women are considered to be the "guardians" of the *Shakti energy.* It is said that the *Shakti's* power is limitless. The moment it is awakened and all the energetic, spiritual, and sexual forces are creatively channeled.

When *Shakti* is awakened in a female, she rises up to meet her male counterpart, *Shiva*. Their energies will merge and will create an alchemical union of bliss and pleasure. In Tantra, the coupling and union of a man and a woman is something sacred. It is a representation of a far greater universal creative process, while the sexual intercourse between lovers simulates the sacred dance of *Shiva* and *Shakti*.

How the Western Culture Revived the Practice of Tantric Sex

Eastern cultures have been practicing sacred sexual traditions for centuries, but they were eventually forgotten over time, because of the cultural changes, religious objections, and political upheavals that occurred. It is truly a great thing that sacred sexual traditions are being revived in the West by incorporating ancient traditions with Western practices and beliefs.

Tantric sex practices were introduced only about a decade ago. Students of meditation and yoga in the Western culture resurrected the practices. Even though sacred sex practices, beliefs, and principles originally came from the East, people from the West offered modern day practices of tantric sex to the public. Here is a brief overview of how tantric sex appeals to people of this generation in the West. It is important to remember that these are generalizations of the Eastern versus Western culture paradigms and should not be viewed as absolutes in any way.

Tantric sex features simple steps that yield "instant" results that sound appealing to Westerners.

Tantric sex allows couples to use their desires. Westerners don't like the idea of denying desires. Therefore, they will find the practice of tantric sex aligns with that thought. Most Westerners like the idea of adapting to the principles in order to achieve higher states.

Anyone can practice tantric sex without joining any religious groups. Westerners often frown at the idea of finding enlightenment and ecstasy by abandoning their faith and beliefs. They tend not to want to join groups that require them to shave their heads, wear godly clothes, and give up worldly goods and practices.

Westerners want to be in control of the important aspects of their lives and have influence over their partners. Tantric sex promotes control by channeling a powerful energy to different parts of the body for specific purposes.

Tantric sex is rooted in the transformation of energy, and Westerners know about the concepts of electronics, physics, and modern technology.

The basis of Western society is individualism, and therefore, tantric sex will appeal to Westerners, because it begins with individual practice before expanding the practice with a partner.

Tantric sex encourages self-discovery, which can be aligned with the Westerners' desire for self-improvement.

The human body is honored and revered when one engages in tantric sex, and Westerners tend to be more focused on their physical appearance as a whole.

Chapter 3:

Practical Ways to Incorporate Tantric Sex Elements Into Your Sex Life

Most of the time, partners sexually interact based on what they are used to doing – *you do me and then I do you, and let's try to have a good experience*. With tantric sex, couples are encouraged to bring a different level of "giving and receiving" to sex.

Work with your partner on improving deep breathing.

It is quite common for one or both partners to zone out during sex. Often times, partners are so focused on their individual desires that they neglect those of their partner. You have learned in the previous chapter that in tantric sex, you have to be mindful of your actions and be in the present moment at all times. This is the most important aspect.

You have to pay attention to what you are experiencing, the pleasure your body is feeling, the way you and your partner are breathing, and how your partner is responding to your touch, because they are all important factors for achieving the most mind-blowing tantric sex.

Begin with the kisses.

Begin with the kisses. Give yourself time to kiss your partner and explore his or her mouth with your tongue, and then let him or her do the same for you. Be in that moment. Feel the kisses. Be aware of what the kisses do to your body. While you are doing the kissing, see how you can still fully give yourself an active role. When it is your turn to receive the kisses from your partner, surrender to the feeling, pleasure, and experience, completely devoid of any inhibitions. Give in!

Give each other a massage for an hour, without sex!

Set aside one or two hours and give each other full body massages, but do this on different days than when you have intercourse. The important step here is that the massage will only have to culminate with genital stimulation minus the intercourse. Take this "activity" to heart. As with the kissing, completely take on the role of giver and discover new ways to pleasure your partner. When you are at the receiving end of the massage, let your partner know how you like this experience.

Surprisingly, this may give each of you new insights as to how you can interact with each other either inside or outside of bed.

Talk about Sex.

Most people, even couples who have long been together and have been having sex for years, consider talking about sex as taboo (but doing the deed isn't). Tantric sex tells you to break the taboo and talk to your partner about sex and how you want him or her to pleasure you and vice versa. Do not be embarrassed to talk about and explore the topic. The two of you are already having sex anyway, so what is there to be shy about?

Explore each other's bodies.

While you are talking about sex, be bolder and
identify your own personal taboos, regarding sex.
Your partner might be obsessing about a position, but
is too embarrassed to ask you to do it with him or her.
You, on the other hand, might want your partner to
do something different. Once you have both talked
about these things, watch how your sexual
intercourse will elevate to the most pleasurable
tantric sex you've ever had.

Try sexual taboos together.

Try sexual taboos together - however, make sure that it is consensual. Once that is established, you can then decide on a fantasy that you'll be bringing to life. For example, you could start with one of you as a sexual slave and try a BDSM scenario. Or, you could create a fantasy that one of you is an attractive professor and the other is a sexy, captivating student.

Trying out sexual taboos isn't wrong. In fact, it could strengthen your intimate bond even further, because you somehow get to try things you hadn't tried before. It's all about exploring your sexuality and making sure that things do not become boring in the bedroom. By doing this together, you get to be closer to each other and realize that there is still a lot of things you two can do to spice up your life as a couple!

Chapter 4:

The Art and Science Behind Tantric Sex

Tantra is actually a spiritual path, wherein specific practices using sounds, movements, breathing, and symbols help quiet the mind and trigger sexual energy between two people. This sexual energy is directed toward the body, so states of consciousness bring you to heightened pleasures that are experienced, not just by the body, but also by the mind and soul.

What many people don't know is that the practices also aim to heal past hurts that are usually stored in the sexual centers of the body. It is important that past hurts are healed, because this will allow the two of you to become fully aware of each other and to be in the moment at your most vulnerable states.

This will, in turn, make it easier to open up to loving and being intimate. If both partners practice the tantric techniques together, then both will feel the powerful energy flowing between the two, which energizes your whole beings and expands your love for one another.

You should also realize that tantric sex is more than just a philosophy — it is actually an art and science. As you may have noticed in earlier chapters, there is a process to this. It's not something you just dive into right away without any direction. Here are a couple of reasons tantric sex is considered a science:

If you may recall, Tantra actually means "technique."

You see, science is concerned with how things should be done, and as aforementioned, each chapter of this book shows various practices you can try in order to make way for tantric sexual experiences.

Doctrine is meaningless.

Again, tantric sex is concerned with the technique and with various methods. It's not an ideology to which one must strictly adhere without any variance.

History tells all.

Tantric sex has been around for centuries. It is something that has kept, and still keeps, a lot of couples' relationships strong and thriving. There is proof that couples who've integrated these practices have seen an improvement in their sex life.

It makes way for change.

Science is all about innovation. It's about finding or making use of things that could help develop one's life for the better. Tantric sex helps you accomplish this as well. Because tantric sex will be a constant work in progress for you, you're not thinking about mastering it; rather, you are focused on improving each time.

The Science of Sacred Sex

So, how does all this occur?

Feel your own sex center and feel the energy that flows there. If you are seated on a chair, then press yourself against it. If you are standing, then simply squeeze the muscles in your buttocks. Tantric traditions say there is a powerful energy generator in the sex center, and it doesn't end with physical pleasure.

Imagine how you'd feel if there were electrical volts surging into your sexual area, then direct that energy to your heart, so you can feel more of the love. You can also direct that energy towards your mind, so you can get the most over-the-top orgasm, thus putting you into a complete state of bliss.

When you perform tantric sex, it should include the practice of the different meditation techniques and exercises, such as yoga, in order to arouse that powerful energy. Channel that energy, cycle that energy with your partner, and send it out into the universe.

Tantric sex is also practiced to gain personal fulfillment, create deeper interpersonal intimacy, and make a connection with the world. You can use the powerful energy you unleash, either for you and your partner's pleasure and bliss during sex, or for complete healing.

Tantric Sex

What does tantric sex do to your body?

The practice of tantric sex allows a balance to be reached between male and female energies.

It allows partners to align their whole being with one another through a divine sexual experience.

Tantric sex leads you toward free expression and helps break down barriers, so you can open up more, not just to your partner, but also to other people.

It makes the sexual union a form of honor to creation and to all animals.

It liberates the soul, so you achieve perfect bliss.

Freeing of the Mind, Body, and Soul

Arguably the most important factor to achieving the benefits of tantric sex is to quiet your mind. Tantric sex tells you to be mindful of the present moment. You are to pay attention to what you are doing. Being aware of the present moment allows both of you to feel a sense of reverence for the experience, leading you to ultimately honor each other's divine beings.

Mindfulness is one of the goals of tantric sex in order for you to let go and release your body. Doing so will enable you to express yourself freely and feel sexual pleasure beyond the physical aspect, down to the deepest recess of your soul. Oftentimes, when you really focus on relaxing your body, you'll realize just how tense your past sexual experiences were.

A Path to Healing

More than sexual pleasure, tantric sex can be used to heal one's mind, body, and spirit. This is useful for both men and women who have suffered from different kinds of abuse, rejection, and loss from previous relationships. Sexual healing is often divided into three steps:

Identifying the past hurts using meditation and sexual stimulation.

Freeing yourself from the hurts by releasing the powerful emotions associated with them.

Replacing all the hurt with positive emotions and experiences.

Chapter 5:

The Effects of Tantric Sex

This chapter discusses the potential effects that practicing tantric sex can have for your life.

It creates Intimacy

Apart from honesty and loyalty, tantric sex also creates intimacy, which you probably know as something that's really important to any form of relationship. Apart from touching each other's bodies and making juices flow together, tantric sex has a lot to do with keeping the two of you bonded together in ways you may have never thought possible. It can revive relationships and even help new ones bloom!

Tantric Sex and Sexual Health

Practicing tantric sex improves sexual health for both men and women. The more you reach orgasmic levels, the more your brain waves are stimulated, thus, altering your body chemistry. Stress and depression are also alleviated. Menstrual cramps, weak immune function, urinary tract problems, and headaches can be reduced with this practice.

Orgasms and the Immune System

Tantric sex focuses on prolonging sexual intercourse, providing deeper intimacy, and improving health. By focusing on your senses, you will notice yourself reaching deeper, more satisfying orgasms. There are some that experience orgasms lasting as long as 20 minutes. Furthermore, prolonged orgasms can help eliminate depression and anxiety.

Some have even claimed that they've experienced "full-body orgasms" after trying tantric sex. In fact, they believed tantric sex made their sexual lives more interesting, and it made sexual intercourse more pleasurable in the eyes of their partner. This is because tantric sex makes sexual energies move, instead of keeping them suppressed. You'll no longer feel as if you're deprived of something; you've instead given yourself permission to tap into deeper parts of your sexuality!

Frequent Orgasms

With improved sexual health, you get to experience more frequent orgasms. Ordinary orgasms usually last a few seconds to a couple of minutes and are often isolated to the genitals only. With tantric sex, however, orgasms involve your whole body, mind, and soul, and they can even last for hours!

Frequent and more powerful tantric orgasms have been found to increase the levels of the hormone, oxytocin, associated with one's personality, social skills, passion, and emotional quotient - all of which can impact your emotions, social life, career, and marriage.

More so, these orgasms are great, because they are said to come from the heart. Sure, it's your genitals that are working, but because you develop a deeper understanding of each other, you see sexual intercourse as something that could really bring you and your partner together.

As partners, you become people who are always in tune with your inner hearts and deepest desires, and not just to what your mind and bodies are telling you. Whether with orgasm or not, you enjoy sex, and sooner or later that, in itself, can bring the most explosive orgasms you can imagine.

The Challenges it Brings

There is nothing worse than a relationship that has already gone stale. Sometimes, this happens because you're both so busy that you no longer have time to just be with each other and try to be intimate without it feeling like a chore.

Tantric sex then seems to be fun, although challenging, because it allows you both to try different positions. It makes you feel like sex is something new; there is no reason for you to feel like your relationship already reached its end.

Sometimes, it's good to encounter challenges in a relationship, because it allows for an opportunity to stimulate the mind and try something out of the ordinary. Then, it doesn't feel like you've hit a rough patch. Rather, it makes you feel that there are actually a lot of things to do; you can always learn something new!

Chapter 6:

Pros and Cons of Tantric Sex

While tantric sex certainly has its share of benefits, there are some potential negatives of which we must be aware. Let's overview the pros and cons here:

Pros

First and foremost, tantric sex is easy to learn. Aside from this book, you can actually join online courses and make use of manuals that will help you understand the subject even further. It's certainly not something that's out of reach to a person searching for information.

Tantric sex is not just about the physical aspect of the sexual act, as you also achieve spiritual rejuvenation. It is like emerging as a new person – refreshed and renewed. This way, you will always be in the moment while having intercourse. You'll learn to take each day as it comes, and you'll be more appreciative of your partner and the kind of relationship the two of you have.

Tantric sex allows you to stop slacking off. It allows you to turn off the TV and not allow your relationship to become boring. It allows you to stop turning your relationship into something that's just based on text or chat messages alone, but something that could really be consummated. Aside from that, it also allows you to be sexually mindful — or to be more attentive and playful with your partner. Then, your sexual experiences will no longer be bland.

In addition, tantric sex also helps you create a sexual atmosphere. For example, you'll now be making use of the following:

The Power of Light

You'd know when to keep it on, off, or just dimmed. You'd know that every type of sexual experience requires proper lighting, and this could help elevate you and your partner's moods.

Aromatherapy

You could also make use of certain scents that could elevate the mood of lovemaking in the bedroom. Samples include jasmine, wild orchid, rose, or vanilla. Sandalwood, musk, and ylang-ylang are helpful, as well (as mentioned earlier).

Music

You could play instrumental music or songs that you
know your partner finds sexy.

Tantric sex also helps you to become more in tune with your surroundings. Aside from being more appreciative of your partner, you'll also get to appreciate your surroundings more, because you know that without it, your sexual experience may not be complete. You'll know that your surroundings have a lot to do with how you feel as a couple. Colors and sounds can seem more vivid. It's like having your own natural high, which is better than any kind of drug.

Tantric sex helps you improve your breathing and physical conditioning. When you practice tantric sex, there are exercises that are similar to yoga. You'll become more in touch with your body in ways that you may have never even thought were possible.

Tantric sex also helps you give up control in a good way. You'll be able to take turns, not only in receiving orgasms, but more in regards to who will lead the way. You get to flow with the rhythm of love. You do not calculate or over-analyze. You enjoy each moment for what it is.

More so, tantric sex allows you to express joy. When that happens, your partner also feels better, because he/she gets to realize that they are able to make you happy and that you also make your partner happy. It's important to be appreciative of each other, because it strengthens your relationship in the long-run.

And of course, most importantly, you'll also realize that sex is actually a divine gift, especially if you both know how to go forth with it. It's not something dirty; it's pure, and it's up to you to let it stay that way. Sex can provide pure ecstasy, and that's something worth longing for.

When you practice tantric sex, you become fully aware as to how your partner is reacting to your stimulations. It allows you to determine what he or she likes, what sets him or her off, and what acts have little effect on him or her. The same also happens with your partner towards you. When you know exactly how to please your partner, your sex life and lovemaking improves substantially.

Cons

The long term health benefits of tantric sex take time to manifest themselves. Initial benefits of bliss and satisfied sexual acts can be considered short-term benefits. The physical pleasure and those moments of continuous orgasms have their limits. So, do not expect your lovemaking to necessarily improve right away.

There are times when tantric sex may seem too challenging. In this case, it takes away the rawness of sex, or the pleasure that you could get from it right away. But then again, you have to realize that since tantric sex is a very complex art, you can't just expect yourself to get it right the first time. You may even feel frustrated, but that's fine because it only means that you care — and you can work on making it better the next time around.

Tantric sex takes a lot of practice to become good, before seeing the "imagined" results. It may take a long time, but ecstatic results will come - you and your partner just have to be patient. Some people get frustrated and quit if they don't see the results initially, but then never see the tremendous benefits down the road.

You see, tantric sex involves a lot of steps. For example, it works on the 80% rule, which means that you have to feel good enough to warrant attention, but not so good that you believe this is the best experience you'll ever have. In short, you have to make sure there's still something to do next time. You have to be good, but not good enough, and that can become complicating to the sexually inexperienced.

There's also the issue of sublimation, or thinking of your body as a vessel that needs energy to flow through it. There are times when you'd probably just want to enjoy sex as it is and not think about energies of any kind. This means that it really does require a lot of practice - and patience, as well.

And of course, there is also the problem of communication. Some couples are too shy, so they don't know how to tell each other what they want to happen in bed. You have to be able to help yourself open up and not be too shy with your partner, so you can work on these sexual issues together - and sometimes, that does not come easy.

Some couples find it difficult to learn and practice tantric sex. Some feel discomfort, because they are not used to openly expressing themselves in terms of sex. Tantric sex requires couples to talk about sex and explore their own physical taboos. For some, this is difficult. It can also be rather time consuming, so for people who are living in the fast lane, they may not be willing to spend the required hours up-front in order to reap more rewards down the line.

Chapter 7:

Differences Between Men and Women

Tantric sex establishes the difference between the female orgasm and the male ejaculation. A male's ejaculation and orgasm may seem to happen simultaneously, but men are actually capable of experiencing orgasms without ejaculating.

For Women

Women can experience orgasms multiple times for as long as it comes. Women are encouraged to explore their sexuality. She is encouraged to tap into the masculine parts of her soul and to feel like the leader, not just the follower.

A woman is encouraged to learn ways of teaching a man how she wants to be pleased in bed. You, as a woman, should take initiative and show your partner that you're not just someone who will give in all the time, but someone who knows what she wants in bed.

The Radiant Light

This is an exercise that will help women get in touch with their tantric sexuality. Imagine yourself as an enlightened being, as a goddess who is in control of what should happen in the bedroom.

Then, imagine yourself floating through a sphere of light, and you're getting your lovemaking energy from the said light. Now, for each lovemaking session, think of that light and remember how strong you are.

Aside from invoking strength, try to radiate some joy from the light. Let that joy envelope you, and make you feel safe. Let that joy bring harmony in your relationship, and let it illuminate every part of your relationship as a couple.

For Men

For men, it can be different. Control of ejaculation is important in tantric sex if couples want to learn to extend the magical and powerful energy of orgasm. Men can experience a series of "mini-orgasms" by simply learning to hold back in a healthy way.

You see, males are encouraged to tap into their feminine, vulnerable sides. It means he doesn't have to act and feel like he's the "alpha male" all the time, who wants emotion-less sex. It's about knowing that sex is sacred, and it could be full of emotions. It should be a symbol of love, rather than a symbol of how you can only overpower and dominate a woman (though there is a time for that as well).

In short, men get to believe that women are also capable of leading sexual relationships; they can be in control of a sexual situation. They can dominate, instead of always being asked to submit. It's a good way to create balance and fun in the bedroom!

This does not mean that men will never ejaculate, but it just requires controlling the climax. The main purpose is to catch the wave of energy and "ride the waves"   without   going   over   the   edge.

Stri Puja

This is an exercise that you can try, and it basically helps shape the spiritual component of tantric sex. It is all about "offering yourself up to the goddess" or the sacred worship of a woman.

In order to do this, it would be good to create something that would resemble an altar. Fill it up with flowers, incense, and gifts. Then, go ahead and use a moist flower to touch the "body" of the goddess. You can perform this on your own body or on the body of your partner.

After that, go and massage her foot with oil and offer her the delicacies you know she likes the most. Kneel and bow before her and go ahead and praise her. This is actually a good challenge for you both, because a woman may feel challenged to embrace her sacredness, while you could then cultivate your appreciation and gratefulness for women — especially your woman!

By trying this exercise, you get to feel more positive about your relationship with your partner, and you get to create arousing sexual intent. Sex may then no longer feel like a chore, and you'll also feel like the woman is actually excited, instead of just pretending to be. In the end, it will provide greater harmony and balance for your relationship over the long-haul.

Gender Equality and Life Source

So, you may be asking: Do these exercises mean that you have to let go of who you really are? That you have to sacrifice your sexuality?

Well, the answer is definitely not. On the contrary, it allows both men and women to get in touch with different facets of their personality. It helps you realize that you are not linear; you cannot just be labeled.

Sure, you love to submit, but can't you dominate as well? Of course you can. You have it in you, and all you have to do is tap into it. Tantric sex allows you to take your time, so you can understand yourself better, instead of just having sex without any form of meaning. It's all about discarding gender stereotypes and honoring polarities that have often been ignored.

What happens when these feminine and masculine polarities come together is a person becomes whole and they begin to understand how sacred sexual intercourse can be. More so, it brings forth an important life source. It makes a person realize that in the future, if he or she decides to be a parent, he/she could love the child in such a way that both father and mother could. This is because aside from sex being enjoyable, the person gets to tap into the heart and gets to understand their partner even further. And clearly, understanding is an essential part of any relationship.

Other Information

The following information might help in your practice:

If you are a man, your pubococcygeal (PC) muscles (from the pubic bone to the tailbone) are your sex muscles. They are the same muscles you use to stop the flow of urine. If your PCs are properly conditioned, then you can delay ejaculation and enjoy sex longer.

Learn to contract your PC muscles at least three times a day, squeezing 20–25 repetitions. You can do this anytime. After one month, you may try to extend the squeezing by holding every contraction for 2 seconds and work your way up to 10 seconds. Once your PCs are conditioned, it is easier to pump during sex without releasing too soon.

You will have to learn to relax during the heightened state of arousal. You need to take it slow when you feel waves of ejaculation. Relax and redirect the energy from your penis and your thoughts to your partner.

When you are performing the sexual act, you have to thrust slowly while allowing your arousal to gradually build. Even before the excitement mounts, pull back, relax, and tighten your PC muscles. Take a deep breath, resume intercourse, and continue to build excitement as you make love.

It takes time, but when you "master" the technique, you and your partner will enjoy tantric sex and develop a deeper connection with each another.

Chapter 8:

The Future of Tantric Sex and Sacred Sexuality

The Tantra is about respect, honor, and healing. Learning and practicing tantric sex allows you to learn to respect and heal yourself.

You have learned that the Tantra and tantric sex can help you heal past hurts and open your heart to create a deeper, more loving relationship with your partner. The Tantra does not make prejudices towards any human being or other living thing. One can express his or her loving energy in all aspects and in any direction, while at the same time, receiving the same.

What is the future of tantric sex? People need to be told that they are loved. Most of them fear they cannot get the love that they can give. The basic teaching of the Tantra is to express your love for the people you care about. The effects of the Tantra go beyond the intimacy you can have with your partner if applied wisely.

Tantra Promoting Tolerance and Diversity

News and tragedies about discrimination in all forms are still rampant today. How does the Tantra relate to this moving forward?

Practicing the tantric lifestyle promotes cooperation and trust, instead of aggression and distrust. People embracing the Tantra lifestyle are capable of breaking the cycle of destruction and dysfunction, by actively fostering a desire to support one another, rather than to destroy.

How Tantric Sex can Help You Heal the World

Communities practicing the Tantra lifestyle usually have a network to come together to promote peace, love, and equality. Even during the height of your sexual arousal, where a powerful energy is being activated, you can easily send out the healing energy of love for the whole world.

Does this make sense? Tantric sex healing the world? But, how is it even possible? Well, if you practice tantric sex, then your overall health is improved, you are less stressed, you are less likely to become depressed, and you have a happier disposition towards life. When you are happy within yourself and your relationship, you become more tolerant of others. When you are more at peace and satisfied with your relationship, you become more willing to treat other people with respect, and you will want to spread the love and happiness you feel.

So, what is in store for sacred sexuality and tantric sex in the future? Tantric practices can help you go beyond the patriarchal world of dominance in which one feels they are superior to others. Instead, you get to enter a world that is full of peace, harmony, and balance – all because you practice tantric sex.

It's safe to say that there really is a future for tantric sex. In fact, it's being practiced by people all over the world, and soon enough, those who'll become informed could really get curious about it and try it out for themselves.

You see, the idea of tantric sex speaks a lot about the future: It ends the divide between gender polarities. It helps one to become more in tune with themselves, their partner, and the world. And in time, they'll realize how being in tune with their sexuality can bring a great deal of peace into their daily lives.

When you learn to love, respect, and honor yourself and your partner, your tantric lifestyle goes beyond your own turf and extends to a larger community and to the whole world, thus creating a world of peace and harmony.

Conclusion

Thank you for reading this! We hope this short, concise book was able to teach you a thing or two about the intriguing topic of tantric sex.

Now that you understand the important factors, regarding tantric sex, you can decide if you want to try it or if you can inform your friends who ask you about it. Plus, a little addition to your knowledge doesn't hurt, right? Our world is becoming increasingly interested in the use of alternate methods of sexual intercourse, especially for those who are not as driven by the physical form of their sexual partner.

If you've learned anything from this book, please take the time to share your thoughts by sending me a message or even posting a review to Amazon.

Thank you and good luck in your journey!

21109810R00083

Printed in Poland
by Amazon Fulfillment
Poland Sp. z o.o., Wrocław